# *P*requel:

Hey, thanks for coming on this journey with me, ya'll ready for this trip? Our travels take us through the mind and across time, places that will seem common and some that will seem, not...so common. This land of dating can be very confusing, misleading and hard to manage. One minute you've found someone to ride out the rest of life adventures, the next your downloading apps and posting single memes. It's a wild ride but I firmly believe that it is worth it. So, if your all buckled in. Here we go....

# Adventure 1:
# Semantics

The prologue:
She and I exchanged information, this is literally the 1$^{st}$ conversation we had.

25:57

> At work or just in life? What else are you up to today?
11:53 AM

I'm at work. I'm going home a bit early after I run a few errands.
12:03 PM

I have to pay camp rent at all the locations
12:03 PM

Get out bills in order
12:04 PM

Our
12:04 PM

> Brooks never really done even when you're not at work you still working if you have any time in between those things maybe we can meet up?
12:04 PM

Are you asking me out?
12:12 PM

> Yes...do you need me to be more formal ?
12:13 PM

Yes please
12:13 PM

> Im strait...
12:16 PM

Enter message

MAID 3

Up for discussion:

If a woman and guy are at a bar, and the guys says to the woman…" drink?" Is she going to say no because he didn't say "I would be honored if you would do me the pleasure in sharing in libation with me?" No, because she wants a drink. I always say, it's not about what a person will or won't do, it's about what a person will or won't do…for you…I promise if the right person asked or suggested the way in which it was suggested here it would not matter at all. Just as an example, I don't mean to insinuate anything about anyone, but take me out of this text convo, insert someone like Drake, Dwayne Johnson, Bradley Cooper anyone like that, you really think she would care about the formality? For that reason, I felt like this is a game she's playing and I chose not to. Did I cut her off too quick?

# Adventure 2:
# Driving...Me Crazy !!!

The prologue:
We exchanged information after a lot of online convo. She stayed on the other side of town, worked and had a child so time was an issue. We would text, try to make plans but, as it happens so often with women who have children, plans changed and get cancelled so up to this point we had never actually met.

**Hey! Whatcha up to?** 1:46 PM

Not much...you ? 1:47 PM

**Same here..looking for sumn to do** 1:48 PM

Off today ? 1:48 PM

**Got off at 1230** 1:48 PM

Herrman park ? 230 ? 1:49 PM

**Oh no...thats too far out** 1:49 PM

**I'll b stuck in traffic** 1:49 PM

I forgor you out in the sticks....where at then ? 1:50 PM

**Ikr...come to Baytown** 2:07 PM

And do what ? 2:08 PM

Enter message

Chill
2:08 PM

Where ?
2:08 PM

Idk...anywhere
2:08 PM

Idk the area....so you gatta pick
2:09 PM

Theres parks..restaurants..bars...all that. I dont really know the area either
2:10 PM

Make plan, let me know
2:10 PM

U coming now?
2:10 PM

Not right this moment....id like to smell better than i do...is that ok ?
2:12 PM

Lol...thats fine BUT i dont have alotta time ya know
2:12 PM

Well go about your day...i wont be there any time soon and im not driving 50 min to an hr to sit outside for 20 min and "chill"

Enter message

MAID 7

Okay whatever 2:18 PM

It doesnt take that long to get here either...and i wasnt gonna b outside
2:19 PM

It doesnt take long to get here...but you didnt wanna make that trip ?
2:20 PM

bye 2:20 PM

Are you reading what your saying ?
2:20 PM

I know what im saying...r u reading it
2:21 PM

You just dont wanna drive ? Aaaahhhh ok
2:21 PM

Im not about to b stuck in traffic...and ur a man...u should want to come to me smh
2:22 PM

And all the traffic right now is going out of the city...people live in baytown...drive into houston...being thr end of the day everyone is going toward bay town...putting ME. In traffic..not you....idk what being a man has to do with anything...at all

Enter message

And all the traffic right now is going out of the city...people live in baytown...drive into houston...being thr end of the day everyone is going toward bay town...putting ME. In traffic..not you....idk what being a man has to do with anything...at all...

2:24 PM

And i said i would b stuck in traffic tryna get back to baytown! But anyway im not about to argue with u

2:26 PM

Its not an argument...its a discussion...

2:27 PM

Well i am bot discussing it either

2:28 PM

Not

2:28 PM

Wow...ok...well how abour what "being a man" has to do with it ?

2:28 PM

Have a good evening.

2:29 PM

Do the same...

2:29 PM

Enter message

Up for discussion:
She got BIG mad huh? We all know the ideology that men plan the date, idk where it came from or why...that's a lie, I do...#patriarchy. But ladies if we are going to come to you, and we've never been there, can you at lease give us something to do? Any suggestion will do. As far "the man thing"...she obviously picked the wrong one to come at with that weak as argument. I've explained before that I'm not into gender roles. We really could have met half way, felt like she wanted me to do all the work. I may have missed out, but we'll never really know.

# Adventure 3:
# A Lose-Lose Situation

The prologue:
Another one that ended almost as soon as it started...

No off Sundays
12:52 PM

I work part time@ a call center n at a barber shop
12:52 PM

What do u do? How many kids u have??
12:53 PM

No kids Full time i work as a case manager for a non profit helping to house families experiencing homelessness...part time i council victims of sexual assault and domestic violence and thier family if they are there...part part part part time (lol) i sing,write, play guitar and a little bass. Ive also been doing air bnb out of my apartment and i just started uber
1:08 PM

Oh ok well i don't want a man that busy lol
1:09 PM

Good luck
1:09 PM

Im not that busy, and people make time for what they want to make time for, but if your not willing to put in that time then...cool, good luck to you as well
1:10 PM

Enter message

Up for discussion:
Man, I can't seem to win for losing. It's actually an ironic twist, almost twilight zone like.... Men are taught one thing if nothing else...Work.... that's basically how society judge's men. One of the 1$^{st}$ question people ask when they talk about a man is "what does he do?" we make judgement off of this, we give some arbitrary status to it. If you do this much work, then you're this kinda man, or if you "only" do that, then you are some other type of man. Usually when I talk about my work women are like, "ohh that's amazing,"" "I admire you," "but, how do you find time to date," which I respond with "people make time for what they want to make time for." This time, not so much. It's frustrating when you think you have at least one thing figured out and then someone comes along and says..."not so fast !!!"

## Adventure 4:
## A Familiar Adventure

The Prologue:
This one was a tough one for our hero, I really liked her, she was funny, and cool, she put up with my gender role-less thoughts and feelings and even shared in some of them. I met her son (spoiled) he and I were cool. I was with her a lot, physical was there, mental was there, all that...then...late one night...

What are we?
1:19 AM

?
1:19 AM

We are the world ...we are the children... we are the way to make a better life so let's start giving
1:22 AM

We are we are the Youth of a Nation
1:23 AM

Got it. Thanks.
1:23 AM

We are Titans Mighty Mighty Titans
1:23 AM

Do you want to have the conversation about where we're going because we can?
1:24 AM

Ummmm yea
1:27 AM

Would you rather call or text?
1:38 AM

My phone has like 2% battery so text
1:38 AM

Enter message

MAID 15

Do you want to go first?

1:40 AM

No

1:40 AM

Then I need more clarity on what you're looking
for if you're asking if mutually exclusive or not if
you're asking me if I'm interested in you I am
aside from that I'm not really sure what you're
looking for as far as like the conversation so
why don't you go first around what you want or
like or don't like

1:41 AM

Exclusive we are not

1:45 AM

Ok. Got my answers.

1:46 AM

Fine....night

1:46 AM

What were you looking for ?

1:52 AM

I wasn't looking for anything specifically but I
wasn't expecting the not exclusive part, mostly
because as far as I know, if we aren't together,
you're at work or with family...but whatever.

Enter message

MAID 16

Up for discussion:
This is a huge one for me, say what you mean, mean what you say...this goes for men and women. But Women asking "What are we?", is about as cliché as we can get. This feeds into my thoughts about the patriarchal standards of dating. Why are you asking ME (one person) what We (two people) are? Why would you give someone else that much power? Had she said, "I want to talk about where this is going", "I'd like for us to be mutual exclusive", I would have GLADLY welcomed that conversation. But instead she decided to ask me and, well...you see where that got her. I am well aware of what Ephesians 5:22 and

Proverbs 18 say, but I really want to see women learn to play a more active role in your relationships and or love lives. If you take nothing else from my adventures, please take that. Needless to say not giving her the answer she wanted, the is the end of the story for our hero.

# Adventure 5:
# Absence Makes the Heart
# Grow...Something...

The prologue:
It was going pretty quick, I'm ok with quick. Most of my actual relationships (mutually exclusive) had quick starts. It seems that when we know, we just know. Though I really wasn't sure of my level of interest yet, we had spent the weekend together basically, but the weekend was over and I was preparing for my work week, plus I had a song I was working on. I was writing songs for the band I'm in, Ambiovox (look us up on Facebook and reverbnation) and I saw the message...

Glad I didn't tell my coworker about you.

11:05 AM

Why ?

11:07 AM

Just not going as I expected.

11:09 AM

What you mean ?

11:09 AM

I felt this weekend we hit it off but the last two days you have been distance and less responsive. I feel like this is maybe not going anywhere.

11:11 AM

Wow, sorry you feel that way...wont waste your time then

11:12 AM

Thx

11:12 AM

Enter message

MAID 20

Thx

11:12 AM

11:12 AM

I guess she was right

11:19 AM

Again, sorry you feel that way, or if you feel i wasted your time or whatever have you...

11:28 AM

I never said that. I said the last couple of days you were distance. I called twice and no response or return call. I texted on Sunday and I only got one answers response.

11:29 AM

But you relise ive known you 5 days including today, and its not even noon...so like 3.5 days and i spent my friday evening... with you... friday night...with you...sat. Morning...with you...sat night...with you...sunday am...with you...excuse me if i havent been at your beck n call from sun. Afternoon until monday night

Enter message

What are you going to post my ass on fb too?

2:08 PM

? What do you mean ?

2:10 PM

Did you not get the pictures?

2:11 PM

Yes, i did...but post your ass ?

2:11 PM

Bye Lucien. Post this shit too. You are an asshole.

2:16 PM

Yes maam

2:16 PM

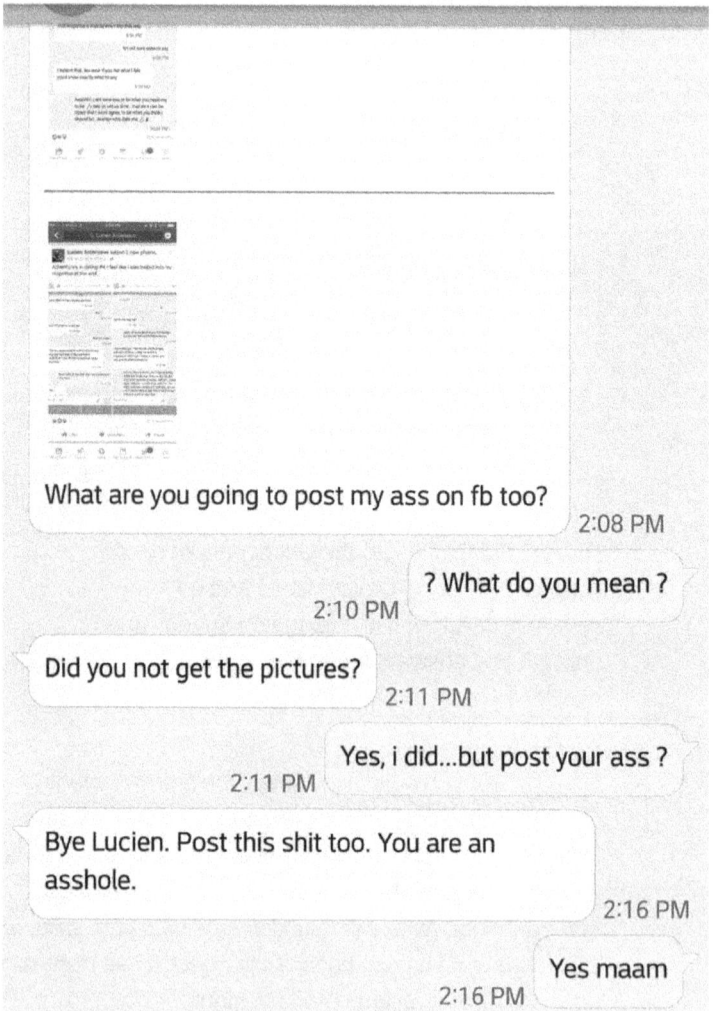

Enter message

Up for discussion:
Man! chill...I'm not sure if you can really see what's happening in the last picture, but apparently she found me on Facebook and saw where I posted the screen shot of the conversation. As you can see from how it ended she wasn't very happy. I'm sure I could have done things differently but it seems like her mind was pretty made up. Well, just another adventure for our hero. Sometimes I wonder...am I the good guy in these stories ? I'm probably biased because it's me. I'm sure this situation happens to women as well, hopefully Vol. II can shed some light on that.

## Adventure 6:
## Tale as Old as Time

The prologue:
This goes back years before I ever moved states. I actually met this woman on the street, not like... homeless...like we were both out one night and met. I fell for her almost instantaneously, it was crazy. She invited me to her town to be her date for a wedding. I came, we went out the night before, the next morning she was acting strange, I tried to talk to her about it but she didn't want to talk, very distant.

I went to take a shower to get ready for the wedding, and when I came out...she was gone. Her cloths, her purse, her car, everything.... gone. I called and called, no answer, eventually I left. I would call again but no answer for days. Actually we didn't talk again till almost a year after. Fast forward a few years later and she decides she want to try again. she realized she was "scared of what she felt." Even going so far to say we might be "soul-mates." Truth is, I felt that when we first met. But time and that wedding situation left a really, really, really sour taste in my mouth and I couldn't see me allowing myself to feel that again. Ever the romantic I decided to see what could be. I did still like her, so we started talking, video chatting, whatever. She came to see me, I helped pay for her flights. Things moved slow...but moved, then this...

I feel like I misinterpreted what was happening between us. The other day when I told you about that thought I'd had, I'm sorry. That's not where you seem to be with me.

9:32 PM

Ah

9:37 PM

That response is exactly why I feel that way.

9:56 PM

Im not sure what to say

9:58 PM

I believe that. Because if you felt what I felt you'd know exactly what to say

9:59 PM

Aaahhh i cant save you or be what you need me to be. ♪♪ tale as old as time...true as it can be. Upset that i wont agree, to be what you think i should be...women who date me ♪♪ 🔥

10:09 PM

Enter message

MAID 26

Up for discussion:
I'm not sure what the take away is here. If there is one, 1stly I'd say stop holding people to standards that you create for them. Maya Angelo said "when someone shows you who they are the...believe them." I'm not saying people can't/don't change but you have to meet them where they are. 2ndly, I don't get the "If you felt what I felt I would know exactly what to say. Is this that "women expect men to read their minds" thing? Lastly, I would say that you have to trust in love some times. It can be the nature of people to get caught up in what THEY want, how THEY feel it should go. We make up all these rules about what we will and won't do. I'm not saying don't have standards but know that you also have to be open to the idea that the one you want, the one you need, may not come in the package you expect, or it might not come on the time you expect it. Our second go around was ok, but not great. A lot of times she was able to make me feel bad

about myself for not being as into as she was. I was being very preciouses and really wasn't sure it would work. I mean we lived 2 states away, she had kids, I wasn't moving to where she was, her moving here seemed unlikely. I don't want to be one of those stories. I'm sure you've heard one (maybe you are one) "Oh, I moved here behind a man/woman, and then we didn't work out, so now I'm just here." I don't want to be that guy. I like to think I really gave it a shot, we had some good times but ultimately I didn't see a future in it. Eventually things died down.

## Adventure 7:
## This $h!t Here...

The prologue:
After exchanging numbers, we saw that we had conflicting schedules, your hero, never being one to give up still tried. Five or so days into talking I asked if I could see her, she was going out with friends but not till later, her plans had her passing on the interstate near my house, so I asked if we could meet up for a second before that. She declined as she didn't want to be late to the party...cool.
Three days after that the same kind of thing happened, she was off but still had to go into work for a coworker's party or, something like that. Again, her jobs location had her having to pass by my place via the interstate ...I asked to see her again, and this was her response....

9:34 PM

You must be looking for a booty call...lol. All power to any woman who prefers to live that way. But I'm looking for something a little different. If you have no interest in dating, I would appreciate it if you would just tell me now.

9:39 PM

What ?

9:39 PM

I tried to see you the same way the other day, it just happened to be earlier

9:40 PM

I didn't ask to come over, or for you to come by me, i ask to meet somewhere. I have pussy...if that's what i wanted i wouldn't need to ask to meet out with you. Is it because i asked you out twice ? What about me, makes you think i need to call you...for a booty call ?

9:43 PM

Enter message

Up for discussion:
GET OVER YOURSELVES!!! I wanted to be gender neutral in most of these stories but this one I knooooow guys will feel me on. Yes... There are some men out there who are just looking to smash (have sex), but there are also some women out there looking for the same thing. Additionally there are women or just looking for someone to feed them, get their phone fixed, pay a bill, all kinda stuff. But if I haven't really shown evidence of being that dude, don't come at me like that. I'm not dumb, stupid or ugly by any means, if sex is what I wanted...well.... you read the adventure....

# Adventure 8:
# Played Yourself

The prologue:
Hardly an adventure, only texted not a lot of convo, was trying to get to know her then...

6:13 PM

There all good

6:13 PM

I have been so resisting the urge to correct your spelling lol

6:14 PM

Keep it up, you can do it

6:14 PM

Ewww stop. But for real, it's so hard....... 'they're' 🙂

6:15 PM

Ok

6:15 PM

Lol you don't like to be corrected

6:16 PM

Well that's not spelling that's grammatical sooooo

6:17 PM

Enter message

Up for discussion:
"If I didn't send for you, don't come for me." This one is more a cautionary tale of how to talk to people (which I am far from an authority on).  My biggest pet peeve is condescension, she really tried to play me. So all of you grammar/spelling "Nazis" out there just, cool it.  I know I'm not the best with spelling or grammar (evidenced by this book) but if you going to come for me, have your stuff in order...THE END

# Adventure 9:
# Played Yourself
# Pt. 2

The prologue:
Different woman from the last adventure of the same title. We had a few conversations, they were kind of blah, I should have known from that. But, I have these theories about dating one of which is the theory of the selves. It talks about how in getting to know someone (form dating or online or meeting in life) there are different selves. There is the "profile self", where you of course highlight the positives and speak highly, then the text/message self where you see more of the personality. But, due to its impersonal nature, can still be hard to learn about a person from it. From there you have the "phone self" which you learn more about a person when they don't have time to think of the perfect response. Next, the "in person self", which is all about the vibe.

here you get to see facial expressions, and mannerisms and all that. Finally, after all that, you get to a more "actual self"; here you start to really understand a person. All these stages are different and in some ways misleading. Someone might be better on the phone than through text. Some might be best in person. I've been in situations where the text was great, the phone was great but in person, the vibe was just...missing in action, just was not there. I myself like to try to skip from the text to the in person stage in the most time efficient way as possible so I'm trying to spent time asap. Anyway...trying to think the best of people I went in for the attempt again, when...

Nada...are you free today ?

4:22 PM

I am what's up

5:43 PM

Trying to see you tonight

5:44 PM

Well what do you have planned

5:57 PM

Pool ?

6:17 PM

Nah I have a bad sinus infection

6:26 PM

Anything else

6:50 PM

Nah im good....hope you feel better

6:54 PM

Enter message

Anything else

6:50 PM

Nah im good....hope you feel better

6:54 PM

Ok

7:09 PM

Kareoke....

7:09 PM

Tonight? That sounds fun

7:12 PM

But....your sinus infection....😐😐😐😐😐

7:12 PM

I am ok tho

7:13 PM

Naw....get your rest....

7:13 PM

Enter message

Up for discussion:
This is more of cautionary tale again, don't be her. If you're not feeling the idea for a date then say that, or suggest something else, again this speaks to being active in the relationship. This one was funny, but low key pissed me off, I feel like this happens a lot, guys let me know if I'm wrong. It's kind of messed up. You want the man to plan the date, and "whatever you want to do" but if it's not something you want to do, things like this happen. And at the same time you're not going to suggest anything. This kind of goes back to an earlier point of its not what a person won't do, it's what they won't do for you. As someone interested in you I am less

concerned with the activity itself then I am the time spent. If she was that interested she would have been down to meet regardless...right? As an aside, because getting to know you is the point of a date to me, Movies and dinner are NOT dates, bowling is ok but it's counterproductive. Your sitting I'm standing, vice versa.

## Adventure 10:
## It Didn't Even Happen

The prologue:
This one hurt because I liked her, a lot, we met and were drawn to each other. I met her family, she met mine. We hung out almost every day and days we didn't we text or call...the ways some would think it should go idealistically. While this was going so great, I had a coworker who was having her own adventures in relationships, she and her partner needed some time apart. She was thinking about moving out but needed some place in the meantime.

I had a 2 bed room apartment so she asked
if she could get that for a week or so while
she figured things out. I wasn't really sure,
and I really wanted some advice and talk it
out with someone, so I turned to someone
whose opinion mattered to me...her....

Congrats...would yoi still come see me if i had a roommate ?

5:47 PM

Roommate?

5:48 PM

Male or female?

5:48 PM

Si

5:48 PM

Fe

5:48 PM

That would be a lil strange Lu
Me there with another woman?

5:49 PM

Is it a friend or family?

5:49 PM

How ? Shes a co-worker and shes gay

Enter message

84 KB

How ? Shes a co-worker and shes gay

5:49 PM

Yeah right Lu, of course she is gay

5:50 PM

???

5:50 PM

Any man would say, a female roommate is gay...

5:51 PM

5:51 PM

And because a man "would say it"....it cant be true ?

5:52 PM

It's possible but, what woman would believe that, u feel me

5:52 PM

I cant control what you (a woman) believes. If

Enter message

And because a man "would say it"....it cant be true ?

5:52 PM

It's possible but, what woman would believe that, u feel me

5:52 PM

I cant control what you (a woman) believes. If you ask me who else im fucking and i say none, 5, 2 10...it dont matter if. You not ganna believe me anyway

5:54 PM

True

5:55 PM

Now yoy not believing me...that's another kind of issue

5:55 PM

Enter message

I've just dealt with a lot of bull shit & rather avoid confusion & drama....
Plus I haven't known u long enough to trust u like that, what if I told u a man was moving in with me tomorrow, would u still come chill with me?

I like things simple & the gay female roommate thing is a bit too much.... but that's your business....

Jan 19 5:59 PM

Yes i would...

Jan 19 6:00 PM

Why?

Jan 19 6:00 PM

Why wouldnt i

Jan 19 6:01 PM

I like hanging out/being around you because...i like hanging out/being around...not because i think im the only guy you talk to

Jan 19 6:02 PM

Enter message

✓　　↶　↷　　Ⓣ　✏️　◇　💬　⋮

Well I won't come over there anymore & u can see me every other weekend when ▄▄▄ is with her dad.. I enjoy being around u too...

But eventually I would like a serious relationship with a man in the future who is looking for a wife...

We are friends & stick buddies
I understand that this is what u want. I'm cool with this for now..
Like u said We don't owe each other loyalty... 🌐

Your welcome to come over next weekend, ▄▄▄ will be with her dad.

Jan 19 6:10 PM

Not sure where in...the fuck...that came from....but ok

Jan 19 6:12 PM

Lol
Just letting u know where I stand Lu

Jan 19 6:13 PM

Thanks

Enter message　　　　　　　📎　　Send

◁　　　○　　　☐

◁　　　○　　　☐

Up for discussion:

<u>IF YOU'RE NOT GOING TO TRUST ME, WE CAN NOT BE TOGETHER</u>.... her being gay should not have even had to be stated. I thought what we had was legit, but how can she act like that. I'm coming to you as someone I care about, so you know what it is. I believe in being as upfront as possible. Could you ever trust a man (or your partner) this much? could I have worded it better? or was it doomed as soon as she asked "male or female?"

# Adventure 11:
# She's Kinda Cold Blooded

The Prologue:
I was going through a rough time, my job was crazy and stressful and I was thinking about finding other employment. My car was in the shop, I still had transportation but it wasn't as...reliable...other stuff. I forget when we met or what I told her, I'm not sure what I said to prompt this...but...I got this message

Ok. Just a fair warning I don't take off my panties after the first couple dates, and I won't ever help you with gas for you to come see me, or wait for you to get on your feet. 2 of the 3 I don't think I need to worry about it. But I'm just going putting it out there. Hope I don't offend you.

9:52 PM

Ok

9:52 PM

Thats unfortunate...

9:53 PM

What is?

9:53 PM

How unatractive that statement makes you

9:54 PM

Unattractive

9:55 PM

Enter message

Up for discussion:

"Hope I didn't Offend you" ? Rule of thumb, if you have to give the caveat of "not to offend' or "I'm not a racist" it's probably because you know it's offensive or racist. I feel like this is one of those things women will read and be like "women really do that????" "What kinda woman is this ???" and the guys will respond "yeeees !!!" "A LOT." Other women will agree with what she said having similar thoughts, though they may not say it. In the end, I suppose you can't really get mad at her for being "honest" even if it's some dumb ideology like this. Well, you know my ideology? If you can't sit with me when I'm down, I can't stand with you when I'm up...ya know ?

# Adventure 12:
# The Ideological Battle

The prologue:
I'll be honest, this is from too long ago, I can't remember why this was even a thing. This issue of gender roles, gender inequality, misogamy and Womanism (different from Feminism) are a corner stone ideas of mine and comes up with women that I date pretty often and pretty early. Whatever I said set something off in her and she wanted to discuss which I'm glad to do. So she says...

I was thinking about our Convo last night. You mentioned that you're still single bc the women that you've met all think the same.

11:18 AM

Do you think your job plays a role in why you feel that way?

11:18 AM

Yes

11:18 AM

So ... You deal with women who were or are involved domestic violence ? Right?

11:22 AM

Yes and homeless

11:23 AM

And most of those women didn't have a say so in their relationship. It was one sided. Their abuser controlled everything. Made every decision for them.

11:26 AM

Enter message

So they lacked the ability to be independent

11:26 AM

Sure...

11:26 AM

So you're aware that you're comparing the women you meet to the women you work with?

11:28 AM

In the way that they are both living in misogynistic societies that oppress them, yes...difference is my clients are looking for ways out of or around those systems, the women i date accept and or like them. Because (as you said its how they were raised or the bible says)

11:33 AM

Understood

11:39 AM

But just because a man leads doesn't mean he'll abuse the power that was agreed for him to have

Enter message

ways out of or around those systems, the women i date accept and or like them. Because (as you said its how they were raised or the bible says)

11:33 AM

Understood

11:39 AM

But just because a man leads doesn't mean he'll abuse the power that was agreed for him to have

11:40 AM

It all boils down to trust and knowledge.

11:41 AM

But why not circumvent that by equal distribution of "power". There was a poet that said woman was made from the rib of man....not his ankle to be beneath him nor his shoulder to be above him...but his rib...to be his equal...so, when im chosing a partner i don't look to lead or be led....

11:49 AM

Enter message

Up for discussion:

I really want women and men to think about, why you think, what you think.... how much of what you think is based on you yourself and how much is based on how you were raised, the country you grow up in, the time you grow up in etc. more and more we see memes or discussions about "making dating great again" and the "pussification" of men, or the loss of masculinity. I don't see all these things as horrible. Not to be redundant and to drive home an earlier idea, maybe if dating progressed more, men can be seen as more than just a debt card and a shield (provide and protect) and women more than a trophy to be hunted, pursued and won by whatever means. Misogamy dictates that women are the lesser, and a man that acts in ways that we associate with women, they are "less than a man." Maybe if men are allowed to be the things we associate with women or as feminine (for all the fucked up reasons that we do) sensitive, nurturing, vulnerable, caring, giving (more than monetarily) men can cry, and express themselves, hurt. Maybe it's the "men need to be MEN" thing that leads to abuse. I can't cry, I can't hurt, but I can be angry... I can push, I can smoke, I can cheat, I can drink I can use my advantages and privileges physically and/or financially."

Womanism (or being a Womanist), for those wondering "is to feminism what purple is to lavender" so stated by Alice walker. One of the ideas of that movement is to address the intersections of oppression that historically aren't addressed by feminism. I'd like to end my adventure with the (para phrased) quote I used in this adventure from Matthew Henry, an author from the 1700's "Woman was made from the rib of man, not is ankle to be beneath him, nor his shoulder to be above him, but his rib, to be his equal." This is what I look for in my adventures, the reason for the quest...I look neither to lead nor be led...I seek partnership, equivocation in as many ways as possible. until the find it...my adventure continues. Wish me luck!!!

From the Author…

I wanted to add that I called my self "The hero" in these stories but that does not make the women in them the villain; I appreciate everyone I have met regardless of if things ended, great or not so great. I believe that every experience is a chance to learn and grow. If nothing else everyone I have and will meet serves to better prepare me for the person I end up with. So in that way, if no other, I am thankful for the women in this book.

Sooooooo what did you think? Did anything stick out? Is there anything you took away from this? have you seen yourself on either side of these adventures? I want to hear from you, thoughts? Questions? Opinions?... Smart ass remarks... I also want to do a volume 2 and I'm looking for contributors. If you're interested, please send an Email to Lucien.arceneaux.chno@gmail.com

www.ingramcontent.com/pod-product-compliance
Lightning Source LLC
Chambersburg PA
CBHW022132280326
41933CB00007B/654